MAKING & USING CARAMEL

Techniques & Recipes for Candies & Other Sweet Goodies

Bill Collins

Storey Publishing

*The mission of Storey Publishing is to serve our customers by
publishing practical information that encourages
personal independence in harmony with the environment.*

Edited by Margaret Sutherland, Mollie Firestone, and Melinda A. Slaving
Series design by Alethea Morrison
Art direction by Jeff Stiefel
Text production by Theresa Wiscovitch
Indexed by Christine R. Lindemer, Boston Road Communications

Cover illustration by © Georgina Luck
Interior illustrations by Elena Bulay

Read all instructions thoroughly and be sure that you know how to safely operate
your equipment before using the techniques or making the recipes in this book.
Always take appropriate safety precautions.

Storey Publishing
210 MASS MoCA Way
North Adams, MA 01247
www.storey.com

Printed in the United States by McNaughton & Gunn, Inc.
10 9 8 7 6 5 4 3 2 1

Library of Congress Cataloging-in-Publication Data is on file

CONTENTS

To Karen,
my favorite recipe tester.

THANKS TO:

My family, friends, and neighbors, who endured all kinds of caramel samples and never complained.

Joan Parker, the world's best literary agent.

Storey Publishing, and their never-ending patience as this book simmered like a fine caramel. In particular, Margaret Sutherland, Mollie Firestone, Nancy Ringer, Emily Spiegelman, and Tina Parent.

Everyone at Mass Appeal at WWLP in Springfield, including Michelle, Seth, Ashley, Denise, Deb, Sarah, Adam, Jason, Corey, Deb, and Mary. You make TV look easy.

The Cooking School at Stonewall Kitchen, in York, Maine.

Dr. Michael Palmer and Robin Broady, who inspire my writing every day.

PART ONE

INTRODUCTION TO CARAMEL

What is caramel? Some people call it a chewy candy. Others describe it as a rich sauce for ice cream, the gooey center of a dark chocolate truffle, or the sweetest and crunchiest version of popcorn. Caramel is all that — and more. No matter how you define it, homemade caramel is both simple and special.

Armed with a digital thermometer, a sturdy pot, and some helpful techniques, you'll be able to create great caramel every time. The caramelizing process itself is simple: you heat sugar to a specific high temperature, so that it turns from light and opaque to a golden color to a deep brown. When you add cream and butter to the cooked sugar, you end up with a confection that's just amazing. But there's no need to stop there — this book will also show you how caramelizing works its magic in pies, cakes, brownies, and even vegetables.

ESSENTIAL EQUIPMENT

YOU WON'T NEED TO BUY any fancy equipment to make caramel. In fact, you may already have everything you need in your kitchen just waiting to be put to work.

Candy Thermometer

To get the desired results when you're making caramel, exact temperatures are important. Too low a temperature and you'll get a dull, semi-tan puddle; too high and your burned, blackened mass will make a rock seem soft in comparison. Using a candy thermometer removes much of the temperature guesswork. My favorite type of candy thermometer is digital. You can get one for less than $25, and it should come with a clip

so you can attach it to the side of the pot and monitor the rising temperature without holding onto the thermometer. Most digital thermometers also come with an alarm; you can set them to beep when your chosen temperature approaches so you know exactly when to take the caramel off the heat. Make sure the tip of the thermometer doesn't rest against the bottom of the pot (the pot itself is hotter than the liquid) or you won't get an accurate temperature reading.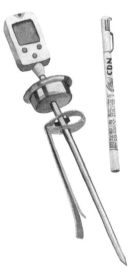

The Stages

When you heat sugar, it's not just "uncooked" and then "cooked" sugar. Sugar goes through several identifiable stages, each with a name and corresponding temperature:

- **Thread:** 230°F to 235°F. This stage rarely comes up in candy making. It's such a low temperature that it mainly applies to a simple syrup, after the sugar has dissolved.

- **Soft ball:** 235°F to 240°F. The sugar will form a mushy, pliable ball. This is the stage for fudge and other confections with a fudge-like texture.

- **Firm ball:** 245°F to 250°F. The sugar will form a firm but still pliable ball. This is the stage for marshmallows.

- **Hard ball:** 250°F to 265°F. The sugar will form long threads. You can form a ball with it, but it will be barely pliable.

- **Soft crack:** 270°F to 290°F. The sugar will form threads that are barely flexible, bending just slightly. This is the stage for butterscotch.

- **Hard crack:** 300°F to 310°F. The sugar will form threads that break when bent. This is the highest temperature you'll want for cooking with sugar; above this point the sugar mixture will burn, so make sure you remove the pan from the heat. This is the temperature for toffee and brittle (the word *brittle* refers to the texture and breakable nature of the candy).

A thermometer is the best way to determine that your caramel has reached the desired temperature. However, it's also possible to test for any particular stage without a thermometer. Simply take a scant half teaspoon of the hot sugar (or sugary mixture) and put it into a glass of very cold water (you can add an ice cube if you don't think the water is cold enough). When it hits the water, the sugar will cool instantly, becoming gooey, hard as a rock, or somewhere in between, depending on its stage of cooking. This clever test will tell you what the texture of the sugar would be if you were to stop the cooking and cool the mixture. If you don't have a thermometer, this is a reliable test for doneness. If you do have a thermometer, then this is a fun way to confirm that your thermometer is correct and that you'll have the desired outcome for the candy's texture.

A Large Heavy-Duty Saucepan or Stockpot

Just as important as the thermometer, a heavy-duty metal pot will evenly heat the caramel to its high temperature. Avoid thin, lightweight pots, which will increase your chances of burning the caramel. Nonstick pans aren't a good choice either, as the nonstick surface often degrades over time — whether from damage or just from wearing out — and this can affect the flavor of the food you're cooking, especially at the high temperatures called for in making caramel.

As for size, I prefer an 8-quart saucepan or stockpot. This may seem large, but when you add the cream to the sugar, the very hot mixture will often bubble up in the pan and instantly (though temporarily) double or triple in volume. Using a large pot reduces the chance of the hot caramel bubbling over and causing injury or cleanup headaches. If you don't have an 8-quart pan, a 4- or 5-quart pan will also work. Just be extra cautious to keep the mixture from bubbling over the sides of the pan.

Stirring Utensils

Heatproof spatula: A spatula is the ideal tool for stirring the caramel and getting every last drop out of the saucepan or bowl. But just because a spatula is made of rubber doesn't mean that it's heatproof. Check the package, or the spatula itself, to make sure it can withstand heat up to at least 400°F.

Wooden spoon: You can use the back of a large wooden spoon (or an offset-handle spatula if you have one) to spread thin mixtures, such as toffee. And if you don't have a heatproof spatula, a wooden spoon can take its place for stirring and scraping. However, wooden spoons can sometimes introduce small amounts of moisture in the middle and later stages of cooking caramel, which can then trigger the creation of sugar crystals and cause your sugar mixture to seize. For this reason, the heatproof spatula is more reliable for making caramels.

Whisk: Called for in many recipes, a whisk will combine the ingredients much better and faster than a heatproof spatula or wooden spoon.

A Pastry Brush

A pastry brush, which is typically used for brushing sauce or an egg wash onto foods, has a special purpose when you're making caramels: when the sugar mixture is boiling, you will use a damp pastry brush to wash down the inside walls of the pan to prevent the sugar from crystalliz-ing and seizing. A traditional bristle brush is a better choice than a silicone brush, which can't hold even a bit of water. Just make sure no bristles come off in the pan.

Parchment and Waxed Paper

In many recipes for baked goods, parchment paper is used interchangeably with waxed paper, usually with similar results. However, when making caramels, I recommend using parch-ment instead of waxed paper to line the pan or baking sheet when required. The high temperature of caramel may cause the waxed paper to soften and melt into the caramel, negatively affecting the flavor. Parchment paper, on the other hand, can withstand the high heat and will not harm the caramel's flavor.

Waxed paper does come in handy for wrapping the individual candies, especially soft caramels, after they have cooled. You can also purchase special caramel packaging materials at hobby stores like A.C. Moore, Michaels, and various online sites.

Kitchen Scale

A kitchen scale isn't crucial, but it will take the guesswork out of some measuring and make your kitchen time a bit shorter. It's usually faster to weigh an ingredient, like butter or chocolate, rather than approximating its weight or measuring it by volume.

THE MAIN INGREDIENTS

THE BASIC INGREDIENTS for making caramel are just as simple as the required equipment. Take a look in your pantry and refrigerator; you might already be fully stocked! When you move beyond making the basic chewy caramel, be sure to read the recipe carefully to see what other ingredients you might need, such as nuts and chocolate.

Sugar

Granulated sugar, also called refined sugar, is the main ingredient in caramels. This is the white table sugar that's commonly used in baking. When subjected to high, steady heat, this white, granular sugar transforms into the browned goo that serves as the foundation of caramels.

Corn syrup helps bring body and sweetness to baking and cooking. Corn syrup is an invert sugar, a combination of fructose and glucose. What this means for making caramels is that corn syrup can also help prevent granulated sugar from crystallizing during the various stages of heating. (Crystallizing almost always leads to the sugar seizing, which leads to you having to start your caramels all over again.) Note that corn syrup is not the same as high-fructose corn syrup (HFCS), and it has not been associated with the many health problems linked with HFCS.

There are two types of corn syrup: light and dark. The main difference is that dark corn syrup also contains a type of molasses, which gives it its color and a slightly sharper flavor. While I prefer light corn syrup, both syrups are considered to be interchangeable for almost all recipes, including candy making.

Brown sugar is a combination of granulated sugar and molasses. Dark brown sugar has more molasses than light brown sugar. I prefer using dark brown sugar for the recipes in this book, but light brown sugar works well too.

Molasses is the syrupy liquid that is left over from the refinement of sugar, when the juice of sugarcane or sugar beets is boiled and the sugar crystals are extracted. Two types of molasses are available in most supermarkets. The most popular kind has been boiled twice; this is what is used in most baking and cooking, including the recipes in this book. Bitter blackstrap molasses has been boiled three times.

Other sweeteners, such as honey, agave, maple syrup, and stevia, are not as commonly used in caramels as the other sugars we've just named. You might experiment with using them for a variety of reasons, including flavor and healthfulness, or even try them as a sugar substitute if you find that you've run out of your intended sugar after you've begun cooking. There are enough variables in flavor, texture, and chemical makeup in each of these alternative sugars to assure one thing: each will bring about a different result if you simply replace one sugar for another in a recipe. For example, corn syrup and maple syrup have similar textures and are both very sweet. However, if you were to use maple syrup in place of corn syrup in your caramel recipe, the flavor and texture of the finished product would be very different. You would probably end up with a maple-flavored caramel — and who knows, it might be a new favorite!

Butter and Cream

Butter and cream are the two key ingredients that give flavor and texture to your caramel. I prefer unsalted butter in all of my cooking, and especially so when making caramel. The main reason is that salted butter can contain a varying amount of salt, and this might make it difficult to get the right amount of saltiness in your food. With caramel, you can't test its saltiness as it finishes cooking because it will have a temperature of around 300°F. (If you think a grilled cheese sandwich can burn your tongue, then you haven't made the absentminded mistake of sampling molten caramel.) That's one reason why you want to be able to control the amount of salt: because the flavor can't be adjusted once the caramel cooks and then cools. Do not try to be clever and take a spoonful of cooked caramel to cool for sampling; while you're attempting to cool it enough that you dare taste it, you run the risk of burning the rest of the caramel that's still in the pot. Cooking caramel needs to be watched very carefully — timing is everything.

Most of the recipes in this book call for heavy cream (which can be used interchangeably with whipping cream). Unlike milk — which can easily scorch and burn, resulting in bad taste and/or undesirable texture — heavy cream can stand up to high cooking temperatures.

Vanilla Extract

For the recipes in this book that call for vanilla extract, use good-quality pure vanilla extract rather than imitation extract. Pure vanilla extract is made by infusing vanilla beans in a solution of alcohol and water. It is expensive because it's labor intensive to harvest the beans and prepare the extract, but it's an ingredient that you don't want to select based on lowest price. Look on the product label for regional names like Bourbon, Madagascar, Tahitian, and Indonesian. Vanilla extracts made with beans sourced from these areas are usually good quality, which will make a big difference in the flavor of your caramel.

Imitation vanilla extract is also readily available, and for a lower price. But its milder flavor will result in an inferior-tasting confection. This is because a key ingredient is synthetic vanillin, which is not as flavorful as natural vanillin. Yes, pure vanilla extract costs noticeably more than imitation extract, but its flavor is vastly better. And because you will use it in such small quantities, you will hardly notice the price difference over time.

Always add vanilla extract at the end of the cooking process. If you add it earlier, the alcohol will cook off, resulting in no vanilla flavor at all — that would make it very expensive indeed.

Salt

The basic function of salt in cooking is to elevate or enhance the flavors of the other ingredients, helping them stand out a bit more. But in recent years, salt has emerged as a revolutionary flavor in its own right. Many candies, including caramel, are enhanced by the addition of salt, and I encourage you to experiment with it. Add a pinch of salt at the end of the cooking process, or use a flaky salt as a flavorful decoration on the candies, such as the chocolate caramel truffle on page 30. But when you add it, add a bit at a time. It's better to add too little the first time than too much. Gradually increase the amount you use until you find the perfect balance.

When making caramels, sea salt will provide the best results because it's the most flavorful. Kosher salt won't be as flavorful, but it's a fine second choice if you don't have any sea salt. Avoid using iodized table salt in caramels. Although it's the most popular salt in the world, it's also the least flavorful. It's worth making that extra trip to the store for sea salt.

SUCCESS WITH CARAMEL 101

THE MAIN THING that can cause a calamitous candy problem when you're making caramel is crystallization. Crystallization is just what it sounds like: as the sugar gets hotter and the liquid in the sugar evaporates, small crystals can form. And if they get in contact with each other, they can quickly become larger, solid chunks of hardened crystal. When this happens, a chain reaction takes place and the sugar quickly goes from a gooey hot mixture to an immovable brick block. It is sometimes possible to halt and reverse the crystallization by adding some corn syrup or a bit of cream and stirring rapidly. But this doesn't always work, and a better goal is to prevent the crystallization from starting in first place.

The key to avoiding crystallization lies in adhering to a few simple rules:

- **Don't stir.** Almost every non-caramel recipe on the planet encourages stirring because stirring helps foods cook evenly and can prevent burning. But when you're caramelizing sugar, stirring gets in the way of proper chemistry. Once the sugar has dissolved and the temperature is rising, any stirring motion will deposit sugar along the sides of the pan, even if you think you're being careful. That sugar, now stuck to the side of the pan and without the liquid in the pan to keep it moving around and heating properly, will quickly lose every last bit of its moisture and start to crystallize. It is okay to gently swirl the pan around to move the bubbling sugar a bit. But no stirring!

- **Once the sugar mixture has come to a boil, wash down the inside walls of the saucepan with a damp pastry brush.** The moisture will keep sugar from sticking to the walls of the pan, which will prevent crystals from forming. Just dip the pastry brush in water so it is more than damp but not dripping wet, and brush it quickly over all the inside walls of the pan.

- **Add a little something to the sugar when you start to cook it.** Generally, there are three basic methods to start caramel: heat only sugar in the pan, heat sugar and water, or heat sugar with some or all of the other ingredients. Crystallization can occur when the hot sugar mixture loses too much moisture too quickly, so it's best not to just heat the sugar alone. Yes, this method works most of the time. Its success is based on the fact that the sugar itself often has just enough liquid to keep the mixture moist so that it can begin caramelizing. But this method can be unpredictable, which is why I don't use it. I prefer to add water (or other ingredients) to the sugar before I start to heat it, which gives me more control over the process. The extra moisture helps ensure that the sugar won't become too dry. This method, combined with washing down the inside of the pan, works very well.

THE BASIC PROCESS IN TEN STEPS

This is the step-by-step process for basic chewy caramel candies (see the recipe on page 23) although these steps also apply to all caramels. The details of a particular recipe may vary, but you'll find that the basic steps, from dissolving the sugar, to boiling it, to bringing it to your desired finished caramel, are universal.

1. Prepare the baking dish by spraying it with cooking spray, lining it with parchment paper, and spraying the parchment with cooking spray.

2. Warm the cream, butter, and salt in a medium saucepan until the butter melts; set aside.

(continued on next page)

3. Bring the sugar mixture to a boil in a large, heavy-duty saucepan. Don't stir the mixture during this step. You can gently swirl the mixture around the pan, but no stirring.

4. When the sugar mixture has reached a boil, wipe down the sides of the pan with a damp pastry brush.

5. Once the sugar mixture has reached its desired temperature, remove the pan from the stove and whisk in the warmed cream and butter mixture.

6. Return the pot to the stove and bring the caramel back to a boil, without stirring.

(continued on next page)

7. When the caramel is the right color/temperature, remove from the heat and whisk in the vanilla.

8. Pour the caramel into the prepared dish.

9. Let cool, then transfer the block of caramel to a cutting board and cut into 1- by 2-inch pieces.

10. Wrap the caramels in strips of waxed paper or special decorative candy wrappers.

Other Helpful Hints

- Safety first! The temperature of the caramel will often be over 300°F. Take care that you and anyone else in the kitchen (especially small children) do not get scalded by the hot mixture. Wear a long-sleeved shirt, and be mindful of the stages and temperature of your caramel. It's crucial to be aware of any other kitchen distractions that can cause you harm.

- Don't dip a spoon, or worse, a finger, into the cooked caramel to sneak a taste. This is not a simmering pot of chicken soup. This is a screaming-hot pot of scorching caramel. Unless you consider removing skin from your tongue and the roof of your mouth to be a weight-loss plan, don't do it.

- Avoid making caramels on a humid day. Humidity can adversely affect the finished candy and prevent it from setting up and achieving the right texture.

- Stay alert while you're cooking, and don't leave the kitchen. While it might seem like the initial stages of heating the sugar take forever, as the temperature rises a matter of seconds can mean the difference between golden brown and burned.

- Premeasure all of your ingredients so they are ready to be added. For example, you might need to add the vanilla and salt when the sugar's temperature is 290°F. If you wait until the temperature gets close, and then you have to reach into the cabinet to grab and measure these ingredients, you'll probably be too late, and you'll have burned the sugar.

- When measuring out corn syrup, thinly coat the measuring cup with butter or cooking spray before pouring in the corn syrup. This will help the syrup pour out faster and completely.
- Be careful when adding cream near the end of the cooking. The molten mixture will bubble up, often to two to three times its volume. This is normal, but you have to be ready for it. Using a larger, heavy-duty pot helps keep it all contained so you won't have hard-to-clean spillovers on your stovetop. If this step makes you nervous, you can remove the pan from the heat while you slowly add the cream. This gives you a bit more control over the process.
- Cleaning up after making caramels is easy with one simple trick: It may look like you need a chisel to remove the cooled coating of caramel from the bottom of the pot, but all you have to do is fill the pot with water and place it on the stove to boil. Once the water boils, the remaining caramel will come right off. If your utensils and tools are covered in caramel, place them into the boiling water and they'll easily come clean, too.
- Have patience. Depending on the amount of cooling time required by your recipe, it might be hours before you can taste the caramel. Remember: it will be worth it!

PART TWO

THE RECIPES

You are now ready to enter the world of making caramel — a delicious place to explore. You can make these recipes exactly as they appear or add your own touches to create your own signature flavors.

CANDIES, BRITTLE, AND TOFFEE

Chewy Caramels

These amazing caramels are perfectly chewy, with the rich taste of butter throughout. You'll never buy a chewy caramel again.

>   1 cup heavy cream
>   4 tablespoons unsalted butter
>   1 teaspoon sea salt
> 1½ cups sugar
>   ¼ cup corn syrup
>   ¼ cup water
>   ½ teaspoon vanilla extract

1. Spray an 8-inch square pan with cooking spray. Line the pan with parchment paper, making sure that it extends by at least 2 inches over two opposite sides of the pan. Spray the parchment paper and then set the pan aside.

2. Combine the cream and butter in a small saucepan and cook over medium heat until the butter melts. Stir in the salt and set the pan aside.

3. Combine the sugar, corn syrup, and water in a large heavy-duty saucepan and bring to a boil over medium-high heat. When the mixture begins to boil, brush the insides of the pan with a damp pastry brush to prevent sugar crystals from forming. Then reduce the heat to medium to keep the sugar

(continued on next page)

mixture at a steady boil until it reaches between 250°F and 325°F, depending on your color preference. At 290°F, the caramels will be a deep amber color; the lower the temperature, the lighter the caramels. You can swirl the mixture around the pan, but do not stir.

4. Remove the pan from the heat and slowly whisk in the cream and butter mixture. The mixture will bubble up quickly; keep whisking until it stops bubbling.

5. Return the pan to the stovetop. Continue cooking over medium-high heat, without stirring, until the temperature reaches 245°F to 250°F, 3 to 5 minutes.

6. Remove the caramel from the heat and whisk in the vanilla.

7. Pour the caramel into the prepared baking dish. Let cool at room temperature for 2 to 8 hours.

8. Once it's cooled, remove the entire block of caramel from the pan and set it on a cutting board. Cut into 1- by 2-inch pieces, or to your desired size. Wrap the caramels in pieces of waxed paper or special decorative candy wrappers. Store at room temperature; they'll keep for about 2 weeks.

Yield: 25–45 pieces

Salted Chocolate Caramels

Chocolate, milk or dark, has a way of elevating a simple, rich caramel. This is a bit of a fancier presentation than the basic chewy caramels. Rather then wrapping these caramels in waxed paper, you can cut them into squares and present them, if you'd like, in a gift box. This candy will be very popular with your friends and family, both for the great look of the gift and for the fabulous flavor of the chocolate caramels.

> 4 cups heavy cream
>
> 1 pound dark or milk chocolate, chopped into chip-sized pieces
>
> 4 cups sugar
>
> 2 cups corn syrup
>
> ¼ cup water
>
> ½ cup (1 stick) unsalted butter, cut into pieces
>
> 2 teaspoons sea salt
>
> Flaky sea salt, for decoration, optional

1. Spray a 10- by 15-inch jelly-roll pan with cooking spray. Line the pan with parchment paper, making sure that it extends by at least 2 inches over two opposite sides of the pan. Spray the parchment paper and then set the pan aside.

2. Combine the cream and chocolate in a medium saucepan and cook over medium heat until the chocolate melts. Turn off the heat but leave the pan on the burner.

3. Combine the sugar, corn syrup, and water in a large heavy-duty saucepan and bring to a boil over medium-high heat. When the mixture begins to boil, brush the insides of the

(continued on next page)

pan with a damp pastry brush to prevent sugar crystals from forming. Then reduce the heat to medium to keep the sugar mixture at a steady boil until it reaches 250°F. You can swirl the mixture around the pan, but do not stir.

4. Remove the pan from the heat and slowly whisk in the cream and chocolate mixture. The contents of the pan will bubble up quickly; continue whisking until the bubbling stops.

5. Return the pan to the stovetop. Continue cooking over medium-high heat, without stirring, until the temperature returns to 250°F.

6. Remove the pan from the heat and whisk in the butter and salt.

7. Pour the mixture into the prepared pan. For a bigger salt flavor, if desired, sprinkle flaky sea salt onto the surface of the caramel as it's starting to cool. It must still be warm, but not extremely hot. After you sprinkle on the salt, gently press it into the surface of the caramel so it will stick to it when the caramel has completely cooled.

8. Let the caramel cool to room temperature, about 5 minutes. Use a knife to make light marks on the surface of the caramel to identify your squares of candy. Do this across both sides, every $1^{1}/_{2}$ inches (or whatever size you'd like the candies to be). Then let the caramels finish cooling, up to 8 hours.

9. Once it's cooled, remove the entire block of caramel from the pan and set it on a cutting board. Following your guide marks, cut the caramels into pieces. Store in an airtight container until you're ready to serve them or package them as a gift.

Yield: about 60 pieces

Rolled Caramel Ganache Truffles

These truffles are made of ganache, the rich-tasting combination of heavy cream and chocolate — and, in this case, caramel — that so often is used as a delicious cake frosting. You can coat the truffles with cocoa powder, chopped nuts, or shredded coconut, or leave the exterior to its simple chocolate decadence.

12	ounces dark chocolate, chopped into chip-sized pieces
¾	cup heavy cream
1	tablespoon unsalted butter
1	cup sugar
4	tablespoons water
1	teaspoon sea salt
1	teaspoon vanilla extract
½–¾	cup coating for truffles (cocoa powder, finely chopped nuts, shredded coconut), optional

1. Place the chopped chocolate in a large heatproof bowl. Set aside.

2. Combine the cream and butter in a small saucepan and cook over medium heat until the butter melts. Turn off the heat but leave the pan on the burner.

(continued on next page)

3. Combine the sugar and water in a large heavy-duty sauce-pan and bring to a boil over medium-high heat. When the mixture begins to boil, brush the insides of the pan with a damp pastry brush to prevent sugar crystals from forming. Then lower the heat to medium to keep the sugar mixture at a steady simmer for 7 to 8 minutes, until the mixture turns amber in color, about 270°F. You can swirl the mixture around the pan, but do not stir.

4. Remove the pan from the heat and slowly whisk in the cream and butter mixture. The contents of the pan will bubble up quickly; continue whisking until the bubbling stops, and then whisk in the salt and vanilla.

5. Pour the hot caramel over the chopped chocolate. Let stand for 5 minutes and then whisk until smooth.

6. Pour the chocolate-caramel mixture into a 9- by 13-inch baking dish and let cool to room temperature for about 20 minutes. Then refrigerate until the ganache thickens, about 1 hour. It might be too dense to scoop after it's cooled in the refrigerator. If this happens, let it sit for 10 to 15 minutes at room temperature, or until it can easily be scooped.

7. When the ganache has cooled and thickened, line a baking sheet with waxed paper. With a teaspoon, scoop enough ganache to form a ball that's about 1 inch in diameter. Then roll it between the palms of your hands to form the ball (it doesn't need to be perfectly round). Try to work quickly

because your body's heat will start to melt the ganache a bit if you take too long. It's fine if this happens, as the ganache will become firm again when it's chilled. If desired, roll the truffle in cocoa powder, nuts, coconut, or your coating of choice. Place the truffle on the waxed paper. Repeat until you've rolled all the truffles.

8. Store the truffles in the fridge, where they will keep for 7 to 10 days.

Yield: about 25 truffles

Molded Chocolate Caramel Truffles with Sea Salt

Molded truffles are so elegant that your friends and family will be awed by your candy-making skills, patience, and generosity. Yes, these do take some time to prepare. But you'll find that everyone's appreciation of these candies makes them well worth the effort.

Molds come in almost unlimited sizes, but I prefer a 6- by 12-inch mold. The size of the cavity, which is what the ganache is poured into, is best at around 1½ by 1½ inches for a square truffle, or around 1½ or 2 inches in diameter if it's round. You don't have to bring a tape measure with you when you buy your molds. Just think of the candies as being one or two bites each. It will be easier to remove the chocolates if you use a heavy-duty plastic mold rather than a silicone or light plastic mold.

Couverture chocolate is the best type of chocolate to use for the outside of the truffles because it contains a higher percentage of cocoa butter. This will produce a smoother and thinner texture, which makes it ideal for pouring and molding.

- 12 ounces dark chocolate, chopped into chip-sized pieces
- ¾ cup heavy cream
- 1 tablespoon unsalted butter
- 1 cup sugar
- 4 tablespoons water
- 2 teaspoons sea salt
- 1 teaspoon vanilla extract
- 1 pound dark couverture chocolate

1. Place the chopped chocolate in a large heatproof bowl. Set aside.

2. Combine the cream and butter in a small saucepan and cook over medium heat until the butter melts. Turn off the heat but leave the pan on the burner.

3. Combine the sugar and water in a large heavy-duty saucepan and bring to a boil over medium-high heat. When the mixture begins to boil, brush the insides of the pan with a damp pastry brush to prevent sugar crystals from forming. Then lower the heat to medium to keep the sugar at a steady boil for 7 to 8 minutes, until it turns amber in color, about 270°F. You can swirl the mixture around the pan, but do not stir.

4. Remove the pan from the heat and slowly whisk in the cream and butter mixture. The contents of the pan will bubble up quickly; keep whisking until it stops bubbling, and then whisk in the salt and vanilla.

5. Pour the hot caramel over the chopped chocolate. Let stand for 5 minutes and then whisk until smooth.

6. Pour the chocolate-caramel mixture into a 9- by 13-inch baking dish and let cool to room temperature, about 15 minutes. Then refrigerate until the ganache thickens, 20 to 30 minutes.

7. While the ganache is cooling, melt and temper the couverture chocolate, following the instructions on page 36.

8. With a ladle, fill the mold's cavities with the tempered couverture chocolate. Once you've filled all the cavities, turn

(continued on next page)

the mold upside down over the bowl that held the melted chocolate, pouring out the excess. Tap the side of the mold with your spatula's handle to make sure no extra chocolate remains. There will be enough chocolate left on the inside of each of the mold's cavities to form a cup. Scrape any drips or smears of chocolate off the top of the mold with a metal spatula. Place the mold in the refrigerator until the chocolate hardens, 10 to 15 minutes.

9. With a teaspoon and, as necessary, your fingers, fill the cavities of the mold almost to the top with ganache. Return the mold to the refrigerator for 20 minutes to help the ganache filling become more firm and solid.

10. After the ganache fillings have firmed up, use a ladle to pour tempered couverture chocolate over each ganache filling. Tap the mold on the counter to remove any air bubbles.

11. Scrape any excess chocolate off the top of the mold with a metal spatula. Chill the mold in the refrigerator until the chocolate is solidly firm, about 20 minutes.

12. Once the chocolates are chilled, turn the mold upside down over a baking sheet, and firmly hit the front edge of the mold onto the countertop. The chocolates will then safely drop out of the molds.

13. Store the truffles in the refrigerator, where they'll keep for 7 to 10 days. Let them rest at room temperature for 30 minutes before serving.

Yield: about 45 truffles

Caramel Turtles

These are the best turtles I've ever had. They're simply the Chewy Caramels (see page 23) with salted pecans and your favorite milk or dark chocolate. It's a good idea to have extra pecans and chocolate on hand, as the caramel yield can vary from batch to batch.

½ cup heavy cream
2 tablespoons unsalted butter
½ teaspoon sea salt
¾ cup sugar
2 tablespoons corn syrup
2 tablespoons water
¼ teaspoon vanilla extract
1½ cups (about 75 pieces) roasted, salted pecan halves
12 ounces dark or milk chocolate
Flaky sea salt, for sprinkling

1. Spray an 8-inch square pan with cooking spray. Line the pan with parchment paper, making sure that it extends by at least 2 inches over two opposite sides of the pan. Spray the parchment paper and then set the pan aside.

(continued on next page)

2. Combine the cream and butter in a small saucepan and cook over medium heat until the butter melts. Stir in the salt and set the pan aside.

3. Combine the sugar, corn syrup, and water in a large heavy-duty saucepan and bring to a boil over medium-high heat. When the mixture begins to boil, brush the insides of the pan with a damp pastry brush to keep sugar crystals from forming. Then reduce the heat to medium to keep the sugar mixture at a steady boil until it turns a deep amber color, about 290°F on a candy thermometer. You can swirl the mixture around the pan, but do not stir.

4. Remove the pan from the heat and slowly whisk in the cream and butter mixture. The mixture will bubble up quickly; keep whisking until it stops bubbling.

5. Return the pan to the stovetop. Continue cooking over medium-high heat, without stirring, until the temperature reaches 245°F to 250°F, 3 to 5 minutes.

6. Remove the pan from the heat and whisk in the vanilla.

7. Arrange the pecan halves in groups of four on the parchment paper to look like a turtle's legs. In other words, place them as though they were on the face on a clock at 1:00, 5:00, 7:00, and 11:00. The "inside" ends can touch each other.

8. With a tablespoon, pour a dollop of warm caramel over each group of pecans, leaving just a bit of the pecans uncovered. Let the caramel cool at room temperature while you prepare the chocolate.

9. Melt and temper the chocolate, following the instructions on the next page.

10. For each turtle, pour a spoonful of the melted chocolate on top of the cooled caramel, covering as much of it as you'd like. Sprinkle a bit of sea salt over the warm chocolate.

11. Let the turtles cool to room temperature. This will take 15 to 20 minutes on the counter or less than 10 minutes in the refrigerator. Store at room temperature; they'll keep for about 2 weeks.

Yield: about 18 turtles

How to Temper Chocolate

To get a great-looking turtle, it's a good idea to temper the chocolate. If you simply melt chocolate, the cocoa fat can separate out, and when the chocolate cools it takes on a dull cast and lacks the crisp snap of great chocolate candy. Tempering — taking the chocolate through a particular temperature curve —helps prevent this. If you pair tempered chocolate with great caramel, your homemade turtles will be spectacular.

To prepare the chocolate, chop about three-quarters of the total amount into small pieces, no larger than chocolate chips. Shave or grate the remaining chocolate, which will help with the tempering.

Fill a saucepan one-quarter to one-third full with water, and heat the water to 140°F. Remove the saucepan from the heat and place a stainless steel bowl over it, suspended above the hot water.

Add the chopped chocolate (not the grated chocolate) to the bowl. Let the chocolate melt, stirring occasionally with a heatproof rubber spatula, until it has completely melted and its temperature hovers around 100°F, 10 to 15 minutes. Slowly stir in the grated chocolate. The chocolate is tempered and ready for the turtles when the temperature drops to about 89°F (for dark chocolate) or 86°F (for milk chocolate).

Peanut Brittle

This recipe is versatile: you can use raw or roasted nuts, salted or unsalted, in whatever combination you like to create your own signature brittle. (Note: If you use raw peanuts, add them at the beginning, with the sugar and corn syrup.) Don't worry if holes or gaps appear while you're spreading the warm brittle mixture on the baking sheet. After the brittle cools and you break it up, the holes won't matter at all.

   1 cup sugar
  ½ cup light corn syrup
  ¼ cup water
  ¼ teaspoon sea salt
  2 tablespoons unsalted butter, cut into small pieces
  1 teaspoon baking soda
  1 cup roasted, salted peanuts
  1 teaspoon vanilla extract

1. Lightly butter or spray a 12- by 18-inch rimmed baking sheet and set aside.

(continued on next page)

2. Combine the sugar, corn syrup, water, and salt in a large heavy-duty saucepan and bring to a boil over medium heat.

3. Once the mixture has come to a boil, place a lid on the pan for 1 minute, to help keep the inside of the pan moist to prevent the sugar from crystallizing. Then remove the lid and place a candy thermometer in the pan. Cook the mixture, stirring occasionally, until it reaches 295°F.

4. Remove the pan from the heat and stir in the butter and baking soda. The mixture will bubble up quickly; keep whisking until it stops bubbling. Then stir in the peanuts and vanilla.

5. Pour the mixture onto the prepared baking sheet and spread it around with a spatula or two forks. It can be as thick or thin as you like. Let cool to room temperature, about 15 minutes.

6. Use your hands to break the brittle up into pieces. Store the brittle in an airtight bag or container at room temperature; it will keep for about 2 weeks.

Yield: about 1 pound

Sesame Brittle

This brittle makes a perfect homemade, nut-free gift. Crunchy brittle is similar to toffee in many ways, but it has significantly less butter, which gives it a unique, lighter flavor.

> 1½ cups whole sesame seeds
> 1 cup sugar
> 1 cup corn syrup
> ¼ cup water
> 2 tablespoons unsalted butter
> 1 teaspoon baking soda
> 1 teaspoon sea salt

1. Preheat the oven to 350°F.

2. Spread the sesame seeds on a 12- by 17-inch rimmed baking sheet. Bake until pale golden brown, about 10 to 12 minutes. After the first 5 minutes, shake the pan every 2 minutes to keep the seeds from burning.

3. Transfer the toasted sesame seeds to a bowl, thoroughly clean the sheet pan, and spray with cooking spray (or coat another 12- by 17-inch baking sheet with cooking spray). Set aside.

4. Combine the sugar, corn syrup, water, and butter in a large heavy-duty saucepan and bring to a boil over medium-high heat. When the mixture begins to boil, brush down the insides of the pan with a damp pastry brush to prevent sugar crystals from forming. Then reduce the heat to medium to

(continued on next page)

keep the sugar at a steady boil until it reaches 300°F. This may take 10 minutes or more. You can swirl the mixture around the pan, but do not stir.

5. Remove the pan from the heat. Stir in the baking soda, salt, and toasted sesame seeds. The mixture will bubble up quickly; keep stirring until it stops bubbling.

6. Pour onto the prepared baking sheet, and spread it out evenly with the back of a wooden spoon or an offset-handle metal spatula, to about ½-inch thickness. Allow to cool completely at room temperature, for 20 to 30 minutes.

7. When it's cool, use your hands to break up the brittle into pieces. Store the brittle in an airtight container or a plastic storage bag at room temperature; it will keep for about 1 week.

Yield: about 1 pound

Toffee with Chocolate and Almonds

Toffee, also known as butter crunch, is an unusual member of the caramel family because it doesn't contain any cream or evaporated milk. It's simply butter, sugar, and more sugar. The end result is a very crunchy, almost tooth-breaking confection.

- 2 cups sugar
- 1½ cups (3 sticks) unsalted butter
- ¼ cup water
- 3 tablespoons light corn syrup
- 1 teaspoon baking soda
- 1 teaspoon sea salt
- 1 teaspoon vanilla extract
- 12 ounces dark or milk chocolate, coarsely chopped
- 2 cups almonds, toasted and finely chopped

1. Spray a 12- by 17-inch rimmed baking sheet with cooking spray and set aside.

2. Combine the sugar, butter, water, and corn syrup in a large heavy-duty saucepan and bring to a boil over medium-high heat. When the mixture begins to boil, brush down the insides of the pan with a damp pastry brush to prevent sugar crystals from forming. Then reduce the heat to medium to keep the sugar mixture at a steady boil until it reaches 285°F. This may take 10 minutes or more. You can swirl the mixture around the pan, but do not stir.

(continued on next page)

3. When the sugar mixture reaches 285°F, remove the pan from the heat and stir in the baking soda, salt, and vanilla. Be careful, as the mixture may bubble up a bit when the baking soda is added; keep stirring until the bubbling stops.

4. Pour the toffee onto the prepared baking sheet, and spread it evenly with the back of a wooden spoon or an offset-handle metal spatula.

5. Scatter the chocolate pieces evenly over the surface of the hot toffee. Let this sit for a few minutes, until the chocolate has melted. Spread the melted chocolate evenly across the entire surface of the toffee.

6. Gently scatter a thin layer of almonds over the melted chocolate. You want a thin layer because only the almonds that are actually touching the chocolate will stick to it. The rest will just fall off.

7. Let the toffee cool at room temperature for 10 to 15 minutes. You can then break it up by hand, and store it in an airtight container or a plastic storage bag at room temperature; it will keep for 7 to 10 days.

Yield: about 2 pounds

Caramel Popcorn with Peanuts

This homemade version of the classic Cracker Jack candy has popcorn and peanuts aplenty. This recipe makes enough for gift bags or movie night at home with friends and family.

3–4 tablespoons canola oil

1 cup popcorn kernels (20 cups popped)

½ cup packed brown sugar

½ cup (1 stick) unsalted butter

½ cup corn syrup

2 tablespoons molasses

2 cups unsalted, roasted peanuts

1 (14-ounce) can sweetened condensed milk

1 teaspoon sea salt

1 teaspoon vanilla extract

1. Preheat the oven to 350°F. Spray two 12- by 18-inch rimmed baking sheets with cooking spray and set aside.

2. Pour enough canola oil into a large soup pot to cover the bottom and set over medium-high heat. Add three kernels of popcorn to the pot and cover. When the kernels pop, add the remaining popcorn and shake the pot to mix the kernels with the oil. Cook, shaking the pan occasionally while the corn is popping, until the pops are a few seconds apart. Transfer the popcorn into a very large bowl.

3. Combine the brown sugar, butter, corn syrup, and molasses in a large heavy-duty saucepan over medium-high heat.

(continued on next page)

Bring to a boil, stirring regularly. Once it boils, cook without stirring until the mixture reaches 260°F on a candy thermometer, about 4 minutes.

4. Remove the pan from the heat and stir in the peanuts. Then stir in the condensed milk, salt, and vanilla.

5. Return the pan to the stovetop over low heat and cook for 2 minutes. Pour the warm caramel and peanut mixture over the popcorn and mix thoroughly with a large spoon. Don't use your hands, as the caramel will still be very hot.

6. Spread the popcorn mixture on the prepared baking sheets.

7. Bake for 15 minutes, stirring at the 7-minute mark. If the two trays do not fit on the same oven rack, so that you have one on an upper rack and one on a lower one, swap them when you stir the mixture.

8. Cool the popcorn in their pans, to room temperature, for 15 to 20 minutes. The popcorn will keep for 5 to 7 days stored in an airtight container or plastic storage bags.

Yield: 2 gallons

SWEET AND SAVORY SAUCES

Caramel Sauce with Sea Salt

Sea salt truly elevates the flavors of this caramel sauce. While this is always a crowd-pleaser when poured over vanilla ice cream, it also makes a perfect dip for fresh apples, strawberries, and bananas. It's the complete dessert.

- 1 cup sugar
- 3 tablespoons water
- ⅛ teaspoon cream of tartar
- ¼ cup unsalted butter, cut into chunks
- ½ cup heavy cream
- ½ teaspoon sea salt
- ½ teaspoon vanilla extract

1. Combine the sugar, water, and cream of tartar in a large heavy-duty saucepan over medium-high heat. Bring the mixture to a boil. Swirl the pan to keep the ingredients moving, but do not stir. Keep at a steady boil until the mixture starts to caramelize and change color, approximately 10 minutes. The temperature will be around 240°F.

2. Once the mixture starts to turn color, stir it with a heatproof rubber spatula or wooden spoon. Then reduce the heat to medium-low and simmer until the sauce turns a deep golden color and the temperature reaches about 290°F.

3. Remove the pan from the heat and whisk in the butter. Then

(continued on next page)

whisk in the cream, salt, and vanilla. The mixture may bubble up quickly; keep whisking until it stops bubbling.

4. Allow the sauce to cool slightly in the pan, approximately 5 minutes, before pouring it into a heat-proof (not plastic) storage container or bowl.

5. Let the sauce cool completely, approximately 1 hour at room temperature, then cover the container and store in the refrigerator, where the sauce will keep for 7 to 10 days. Gently warm before using.

Yield: about 1½ cups

Flavoring Your Caramel Sauce

You can change the flavor of your caramel sauce with just a tablespoon or two of the ingredients listed here. Some flavors may vary in intensity, so adjust accordingly. Don't add these flavors until the end of the cooking, or else the high heat may dilute them.

- **Bourbon:** Add 1 tablespoon (use small-batch artisan bourbon if possible).

- **Hazelnut:** Add 1 tablespoon of Frangelico liqueur or 1 tablespoon of hazelnut extract.

- **Orange:** Add 2 tablespoons of orange zest, or 1 tablespoon of zest and 1 tablespoon of orange extract.

- **Coffee:** Add 3 tablespoons of brewed espresso and 1 tablespoon of Kahlua liqueur.

- **Balsamic:** Add 1 tablespoon of a 15- to 18-year-old balsamic. Or cook down ¼ cup of a younger balsamic in a saucepan until it is reduced to 1½ tablespoons, and add that to your sauce.

Butterscotch Sauce

This sauce is a sundae game-changer. It pairs so well with vanilla ice cream, whipped cream, chopped walnuts, and a cherry that you'll swear you're sitting in an old-time ice cream parlor. Its flavor is a bit sharper than the caramel sauce with sea salt due to the brown sugar in the recipe.

    ½ cup (1 stick) unsalted butter
    1 cup packed brown sugar
    1 cup heavy cream
    1 teaspoon sea salt
    2 teaspoons vanilla extract

1. Melt the butter in a heavy-duty saucepan over medium heat. Add the brown sugar, cream, and salt, and whisk until the ingredients are well blended.

2. Bring to a gentle boil and cook for 5 minutes, stirring occasionally.

(continued on next page)

3. Remove from the heat and stir in the vanilla.

4. Let the sauce cool slightly in pan, 5 to 10 minutes, before pouring it into a heat-proof (not plastic) storage container or a bowl.

5. Let the sauce cool completely, then cover the container and store in the refrigerator, where the sauce will keep for 5 to 7 days. Gently warm before using.

Yield: about 1½ cups

Dulce de Leche

Dulce de leche is sweetened condensed milk that's been slowly cooked until the sugars caramelize. The resulting sauce has a pudding-like texture and a rich sweetness that just melts in your mouth. You can eat it on its own or use it in other recipes, like brownies (see page 61) or chocolate candy. Remember that sweetened condensed milk is not the same as evaporated milk. If you use evaporated milk to make dulce de leche, you'll just end up with cooked milk. And plenty of disappointment.

Store-bought dulce de leche is available — and quite tasty — but there's really no reason not to make your own. This is my favorite recipe. It does require some time for baking and cooling, but the hands-on effort is minimal.

> 1 (14-ounce) can sweetened condensed milk
> Pinch of sea salt

1. Preheat the oven to 425°F.

2. Pour the sweetened condensed milk into a glass pie plate or shallow glass baking dish. Stir in the salt. Cover as tightly as possible with aluminum foil.

3. Set the pie plate in a larger roasting pan. Pour hot water into the roasting pan until it reaches halfway up the sides of the pie plate.

(continued on next page)

4. Bake for 1 to $1^{1}/_{4}$ hours. After 30 minutes, check that there's enough water in the roasting pan, and add more if needed. Continue checking the water level every 15 minutes.

5. Once the dulce de leche is golden brown, remove it from the oven and let it cool in the pan at room temperature for 5 minutes. Then whisk it until it's smooth, and continue cooling to room temperature.

6. Store the sauce in the refrigerator, where it will keep for up to 1 week. Use it chilled, or gently warm it in a water bath or a microwave oven.

Yield: about 1 cup

Asian BBQ Sauce

This sauce is perfectly balanced between sweet and mildly spicy, with a hint of citrus. It's great with your favorite chicken dishes, from wings to drumsticks to boneless breasts, whether baked, grilled, or roasted. It's great all year round.

> ½ cup sugar
> ¼ cup water
> ¼ cup fish sauce
> 2 tablespoons chili sauce (such as Sriracha), or to taste
> Juice of 1 lime
> 2 cloves garlic, minced

1. Combine the sugar and water in a heavy-duty saucepan over medium-high heat. Cook, stirring occasionally and brushing down the insides of the pan with a pastry brush dipped in water, until the sugar mixture comes to a boil.

2. Turn down the heat and simmer the sugar mixture for 10 to 15 minutes, until it turns an amber color.

3. Remove the saucepan from the heat and carefully stir in the fish sauce, chili sauce, lime juice, and garlic.

4. Return the pan to the stovetop over medium heat and simmer for 10 minutes.

5. Store in the refrigerator, where the sauce will keep for up to 2 weeks.

Yield: about 1 cup

PIES, CAKES, AND OTHER DESSERTS

Pecan Pie

This recipe differs from the other caramel recipes in that the caramel-izing of the butter and brown sugar takes place in the oven, while the pie is baking, and not on the stovetop. The results are spectacular! You can use a store-bought pie crust if you wish, but it won't taste as good a homemade crust and you won't get the same bragging rights. For a fun nod to its traditional Southern origins, you can bake and serve this from a cast-iron skillet instead of a pie plate.

Pie Dough

- ¾ cup all-purpose flour, sifted
- ½ teaspoon salt
- 4½ tablespoons cold unsalted butter, cut into 4 to 6 pieces
- 2 tablespoons ice water

Filling

- 4 eggs
- 1 cup light corn syrup
- ⅓ cup packed light brown sugar
- ¼ cup granulated sugar
- 4 tablespoons unsalted butter, melted
- 1 teaspoon sea salt
- 1 teaspoon vanilla extract
- 3 cups pecan halves

For Serving

Vanilla ice cream or whipped cream

1. Combine the flour and salt in the bowl of a food processor and pulse briefly to mix.

2. Add the butter and pulse until the butter is broken up into lumps about the size of small peas.

3. Add the water, $1/2$ tablespoon at a time, pulsing as you go, until the mixture has a barely sticky, doughlike texture.

4. Transfer the mixture to a bowl and gently work the dough with your hands until it forms a firm ball. Shape it into a disk, cover it in plastic wrap, and chill in the refrigerator for at least 1 hour.

5. Preheat the oven to 375°F. Set the rack in the lowest position in the oven.

6. Remove the dough from the refrigerator and let sit at room temperature for 5 minutes. On a floured work surface, use a rolling pin to roll out the dough into a circle about 13 inches in diameter.

7. Gently fold the dough circle in half, and then in half again, so it looks like a quarter wedge of a circle. Center the point of the wedge in a 10-inch pie plate and gently unfold the dough.

8. With kitchen scissors or a paring knife, trim the dough so that just 1 inch hangs over the sides. Fold the overhanging dough under itself to form a rim. Crimp this rim between your thumb and forefinger to form a patterned edge around the edges of the pie plate.

(continued on next page)

9. Bake the pie crust for 5 minutes, then remove it from the oven and set it aside. This is not prebaking the crust but giving it a bit of a head start for a very wet pie filling.

10. Reduce the oven temperature to 350 degrees. To make the filling, combine the eggs, corn syrup, brown sugar, granulated sugar, butter, salt, and vanilla in a large bowl. Whisk until smooth. Stir in the pecans.

11. Pour the mixture into the pie crust. Place the pie plate on a rimmed baking sheet; this will catch any gooey spillover from the pie while it's baking.

12. Bake for 50 to 60 minutes, or until the filling jiggles just slightly in the center when gently shaken.

13. Let the pie cool completely at room temperature, approximately 2 hours, before serving. Serve with vanilla ice cream or whipped cream.

Yield: 12–16 slices

Caramel Apple and Cranberry Cobbler

Adding sweet caramel and tart cranberries to a traditional apple cobbler yields fantastic results — the perfect ending to a meal. Make this a gluten-free dessert by eliminating the flour and doubling the oats (just be sure the oats are gluten-free).

8–10 Golden Delicious apples, peeled and sliced
1 cup fresh cranberries, uncooked
½ cup granulated sugar
1 tablespoon instant tapioca
½ teaspoon ground cinnamon
⅛ teaspoon ground nutmeg
⅛ teaspoon salt
3 tablespoons cold unsalted butter, cut into small pieces
½ cup packed brown sugar
½ cup all-purpose flour, sifted
¼ cup rolled (old-fashioned) oats, ground in a food processor
¾ cup Caramel Sauce with Sea Salt (see page 45)
Vanilla ice cream or cheddar cheese, for serving

1. Preheat the oven to 350°F. Butter or spray a 9- by 13-inch baking dish.

2. Combine the apples, cranberries, granulated sugar, tapioca, cinnamon, nutmeg, and salt in the prepared baking dish and gently toss to mix.

(continued on next page)

3. Combine the butter, brown sugar, flour, and oats with your hands or a pastry cutter until the butter is the size of small peas. If you use a food processor, process the oats first and then add the other ingredients. Use the pulse-chop setting to get the right texture.

4. Warm the caramel sauce, in either a double boiler or a microwave oven, to make it easier to pour. Pour the sauce evenly over the apple mixture.

5. Sprinkle the oat and butter topping over the apples.

6. Bake for 30 to 45 minutes, or until the apples are cooked through and the mixture is bubbling.

7. Serve with vanilla ice cream (a classic!) or a wedge of cheddar cheese (a New England classic!).

Yield: about 8 servings

Pineapple Upside-Down Cake

This traditional cake dates back to the 1920s and is still associated with classic midcentury home cooking. It is best served warm, while the caramelized topping is still gooey. Canned pineapple slices will look nice, but the taste is more vibrant if you use fresh pineapple. And the maraschino cherries add a bit of color and a hint of nostalgia.

Topping

¾   cup packed light brown sugar

4   tablespoons unsalted butter, cut into small pieces

1   medium pineapple (peeled, quartered, cored, and sliced ¼ inch thick; see the box on page 60

Maraschino cherries, optional

Cake Batter

1½ cups all-purpose flour

2   teaspoons baking powder

¼   teaspoon salt

1   cup granulated sugar

½   cup (1 stick) unsalted butter, at room temperature

1   teaspoon vanilla extract

2   eggs, separated

½   cup buttermilk (see Note on next page)

For Serving

Whipped cream or vanilla ice cream

(continued on next page)

Note: If you don't have buttermilk, you can easily make some with whole milk and white distilled vinegar. Just pour 1½ teaspoons of vinegar into a measuring cup, then add enough milk to bring the total volume to ½ cup. Let this sit at room temperature for 10 minutes before you bake with it.

1. Preheat the oven to 350°F. Butter or spray a 9-inch round cake pan with 3-inch sides, a springform pan, or a well-seasoned cast-iron skillet. Set aside. (If you use a cast-iron skillet, you can prepare the topping in the pan and just set it aside while you prepare the cake batter.)

2. For the topping, combine the brown sugar and butter in a large heavy-duty saucepan over medium heat. Cook until the butter has melted and the sugar has dissolved. Keep cooking for 3 to 5 more minutes, without stirring, until small bubbles appear on the sides of the pan. Remove from the heat and pour the sugar mixture into the prepared cake pan.

3. Arrange the pineapple slices in tight, concentric circles on top of the caramelized sugar. Arrange the Maraschino cherries, if using, wherever you'd like. Set the cake pan aside.

4. To make the cake batter, whisk together the flour, baking powder, and salt in a large bowl.

5. Beat together the granulated sugar and butter in the bowl of an electric mixer until light and fluffy, about 2 minutes. Mix in the vanilla. Then beat in the egg yolks, one at a time, scraping down the sides of the bowl as needed.

6. Add the flour in three batches, alternating with the buttermilk, and starting and finishing with the flour. (That would be one-third of the flour, followed by half of the buttermilk, then another third of the flour, then the rest of the buttermilk, and finally the rest of the flour.)

7. In a separate bowl, use an electric mixer to beat the egg whites until firm peaks form. Carefully fold the whites into the butter and flour mixture. Don't forcefully beat in the egg whites because that will remove the air that you just beat into them.

8. Carefully pour the batter into the cake pan, over the pineapple. Be gentle so the batter doesn't shift the pineapple. Smooth the top so the batter is evenly distributed.

9. Bake for 45 to 55 minutes, or until a cake tester or toothpick inserted into the center of the cake comes out clean. When done, the cake will be browned and starting to pull away from the sides of the pan.

10. Let the cake cool in its pan on a baking rack for 10 minutes. Then run a paring knife around the sides of the pan to help release the cake. Invert a cake stand or large platter on top of the cake and carefully turn it over. Let the cake sit in its pan on the stand or platter for 2 minutes, to help settle the caramel topping.

(continued on next page)

11. Remove the pan. A few pieces of pineapple may stick to the pan; just pop them back onto the cake. Serve warm, with freshly whipped cream or vanilla ice cream.

Yield: 8–16 servings

How to Cut Up a Fresh Pineapple

1. Place the pineapple on a cutting board and use a sharp knife to cut off both ends. Position the pineapple so it stands upright. Slice down, between the skin and fruit, to remove the skin all around the fruit.

2. With the pineapple still upright, cut the pineapple in half by cutting straight down through the core. Lay the two halves with their flat side down on the board, and cut through to the core again. You now have four mostly rectangular pieces.

3. Place each piece on the cutting board, lengthwise, with a flat side facing down. With a chef's knife placed at an angle towards the board, carefully slice down to remove the core.

4. Cut up each piece as desired.

Dulce de Leche Brownies

This dessert is the perfect combination of two of the sweetest tastes around: a rich brownie and a rich sauce. You may want to skip dinner and jump right into this dessert. The chocolate syrup for this recipe can be any kind that you want, including your childhood favorite that went into your chocolate milk.

- 6 ounces semisweet chocolate
- ¼ cup chocolate syrup
- ½ cup (1 stick) unsalted butter, at room temperature
- 2 eggs, lightly beaten
- 1 teaspoon vanilla extract
- ¾ cup sugar
- ½ cup all-purpose flour
  Pinch of salt
- 1 cup chopped walnuts, optional
- 1 cup dulce de leche (see page 49)

1. Preheat the oven to 350°F. Butter and flour an 8-inch square pan. Set it aside.

2. Melt the chocolate in a double boiler. Add the syrup and stir well. Remove the pan from the heat, add the butter, and stir until the mixture is smooth. Add the eggs and vanilla and mix thoroughly.

3. Combine the sugar, flour, and salt in a mixing bowl and whisk together. Add the sugar mixture to the chocolate mixture and blend thoroughly. Stir in the walnuts, if using.

(continued on next page)

4. Pour half of the batter into the prepared pan, along with all but a few tablespoons of the dulce de leche. Do not stir. Add the remaining brownie batter and gently spread it on top of the dulce de leche. Try to avoid moving the dulce de leche too much. Scatter the remaining dulce de leche on top.

5. Bake for about 30 minutes, until just cooked; a cake tester or toothpick inserted in the center of the brownies will be moist.

6. Let the brownies cool for 5 minutes before cutting them with a serrated knife (I suggest cutting them no larger than 2-inch squares as they're very rich). If you wait until they're completely cool the top will get crusty and they won't cut cleanly.

Yield: about 16 servings

Crème Brulée

Crème brulée is unique among caramel recipes because you caramelize the sugar with a butane torch (available at most hardware stores) or the broiler in your oven, rather than heating it in a saucepan. This recipe is for classic crème brulée, but for an interesting twist try adding 2 tablespoons of Frangelico liqueur (hazelnut flavor), Amaretto liqueur (almond), Sabra liqueur (orange and chocolate), or key lime juice for a Southern key lime brulée. Add these liquids after you remove the mixture from the heat, and before you strain it.

You will need 4 ramekins or wide custard cups (approx 3/4 cup each) as well as a large roasting pan.

2	cups heavy cream
5	egg yolks
11	tablespoons sugar
1	tablespoon vanilla extract

1. Preheat the oven to 325°F.

2. In a saucepan over a medium-high heat, scald the cream by heating it until it's almost simmering, 180 degrees.

3. While the cream is heating, whisk the yolks plus 3 tablespoons of the sugar in a large bowl until the yolks get a bit thick.

4. When the cream is scalded, slowly whisk it into the yolk mixture. Stir in the vanilla.

(continued on next page)

5. Pour the mixture through a strainer (to get rid of any heated egg bits) and into a pitcher (or any container with a spout). Then divide the mixture evenly among the four ramekins.

6. Set the ramekins in a roasting pan. Pour enough boiling water into the pan to come halfway up the sides of the ramekins. Be careful not to splash water into the custards. Place the pan in the oven and bake for 20 to 25 minutes, or until the custards are just set (they should jiggle a bit when gently shaken) and a skin starts to form on top.

7. Carefully remove the roasting pan from the oven. With tongs and a flat metal spatula, carefully remove the ramekins from the pan and set on a cooling rack. Let the ramekins cool for 1 hour. Then cover with plastic and refrigerate until cold, at least 2 hours and up to overnight.

8. About 10 minutes before serving the crème brulée, pull the custards out of the refrigerator. If you're going to caramelize the sugar topping under your broiler, preheat it now, and set the top rack in the upper two-thirds of the oven.

9. Sprinkle the remaining 8 tablespoons sugar evenly over the top of the custards, using about 2 tablespoons per ramekin.

10. To caramelize the sugar with a butane torch, carefully turn the flame directly onto the sugar. In moments, it will start to bubble and turn brown. Brown the whole top of each custard. If you don't have a torch, carefully place the ramekins under the broiler, on the top rack, and broil until the sugar turns brown, approximately 3 minutes. Remove the ramekins from the oven as soon as the topping is browned; you don't want to let the custard get hot and start to cook.

11. Let the custards cool for a few minutes before serving. Once cool, the caramelized sugar topping will be crunchy. Serve without a garnish or with a few fresh berries or freshly whipped cream.

Yield: 4 servings

Classic Crème Caramel

A crème caramel has a base of caramel with a vanilla custard baked on top. It's then turned over, like a pineapple upside-down cake, and served with the caramel on top. This rich dessert has such a reputation for elegance that your guests will think you slaved over it for hours, but it is really so simple to prepare.

You will need six 6-ounce ramekins or eight 4-ounce ramekins, as well as a large roasting pan. If you want to make one large crème caramel, use a 1-quart soufflé dish and bake it in a hot water bath for 40 to 50 minutes.

1½	cups sugar
¼	cup water
2	eggs plus 3 egg yolks
¼	teaspoon sea salt
3	cups whole milk
2	teaspoons vanilla extract
	Fresh berries and whipped cream, for serving, optional

1. Preheat the oven to 325°F.

2. Combine 1 cup of the sugar and the water in a small heavy-duty saucepan over medium-high heat. Bring to a boil, stirring occasionally. Reduce the heat as needed to keep the sugar mixture at a steady boil. You can swirl the mixture around the pan, but do not stir. Cook until the mixture starts to turn amber in color, 5 to 8 minutes. Cook for just another minute, if that long, until the color deepens a bit. It will be around 300°F. Then remove from the heat.

3. Divide the caramel evenly among the ramekins. Set aside to cool to room temperature.

4. Whisk together the whole eggs and yolks, salt, and remaining $1/2$ cup sugar in a medium bowl. Set aside.

5. Heat the milk until it's hot, but not boiling, in a medium heavy-duty saucepan over medium heat. Then slowly whisk it into the egg mixture. Stir in the vanilla.

6. Pour the mixture through a strainer (to get rid of any heated egg bits) and into a pitcher (or any container with a spout). Then divide the custard evenly among the ramekins.

7. Set the ramekins in a roasting pan. Pour enough boiling water into the pan to come halfway up the sides of the ramekins. Be careful not to splash water into the custards. Place the pan in the oven and bake for 30 to 35 minutes, until the custards are just set (they should still jiggle a bit when gently shaken).

(continued on next page)

8. With tongs and a flat metal spatula, carefully remove the ramekins from the pan and set on a cooling rack. Let cool at room temperature for 1 hour. Then cover with plastic and refrigerate until cold, at least 2 hours and up to overnight.

9. About 10 minutes before serving the crème caramel, pull the ramekins out of the refrigerator. To serve, carefully run a paring knife around the inside of each ramekin. Invert a plate on top of each ramekin and turn them both over, so the ramekin is now upside down on the plate. Gently wiggle and shake the ramekin to encourage the custard to drop out. Serve with fresh berries and whipped cream, if desired.

Yield: 6–8 servings

Bananas Foster

This classic New Orleans dessert comes together so easily and quickly that you don't have to prepare it in advance. The "caramel" factor comes from the sweet, rich sauce of butter and brown sugar. In the unlikely event that you have any leftovers, bananas Foster makes a perfect topping for breakfast pancakes.

½	cup packed brown sugar
4	tablespoons unsalted butter
4–6	firm bananas, sliced in half lengthwise, or cut on the bias into ½-inch thick slices
1	tablespoon freshly squeezed lemon juice
¼	cup rum or brandy
	Vanilla ice cream, for serving

1. Combine the brown sugar and butter in a large skillet over medium heat. Stir until the butter melts and the sugar has dissolved. Reduce the heat to medium-low and cook, without stirring, for 2 minutes.

2. Add the bananas. Cook, continuously spooning the sugar mixture over the bananas, until the bananas are heated through. The edges of the bananas will start to degrade, becoming a bit rounded. While the bananas are heating, add the lemon juice.

(continued on next page)

3. When the bananas are heated through, add the rum to the pan and gently simmer for 1 minute. At this point you can ignite the rum, if you wish. Be very careful if you do (see Rules for Flambé, below).

4. Remove from the heat and serve immediately, with ice cream.

Yield: 6 servings

....

Rules for Flambé

- Ignore all distractions and put down your phone. After all, you're playing with fire.

- Keep the lid for the pan immediately at hand, to cover the pan and extinguish the fire if necessary.

- If you have a hood vent, make sure the fan is off, so it won't fan the flames.

- To ignite the rum, use a "fire starter" (a long lighter) instead of matches, which are too short and increase the risk of burning your fingers.

- If you're using a gas stove, remove the pan from the burner before you add the rum. Pour in the rum and put the bottle down before you return the pan to the burner. This helps prevent flare-ups caused by the alcohol in the pan.

- After 20 to 30 seconds, the flame will likely fade out on its own. If you want to extinguish the flame, place the lid on the pan. Never blow on the flame like a candle to extinguish it, as that can take the fire outside of the pan.

....

Butterscotch Oatmeal-Walnut Cookies

This twist on an oatmeal chocolate chip cookie gets its "oomph" from the rich, homemade butterscotch. You can prepare the butterscotch chips 1 week ahead. You'll never buy butterscotch again!

Butterscotch Chips

- 1 cup (2 sticks) unsalted butter
- 1 cup packed brown sugar
- 1 teaspoon sea salt
- 1 teaspoon vanilla extract

Cookie

- 1 cup (2 sticks) unsalted butter
- 1 cup packed brown sugar
- 1 cup granulated sugar
- 2 eggs
- 2 tablespoons milk (whole, low-fat, or skim)
- 2 teaspoons vanilla extract
- 2 cups all-purpose flour, sifted
- 1 teaspoon baking powder
- 1 teaspoon baking soda
- 1 teaspoon salt
- 2 cups quick-cooking or rolled (old-fashioned) oats
- 2 cups butterscotch chips
- 1 cup walnuts, coarsely chopped

(continued on next page)

1. To make the butterscotch chips, line a 10- by 15-inch jelly-roll pan with parchment paper, making sure that it extends by at least 2 inches over two opposite sides of the pan. Set aside.

2. Melt the butter and brown sugar in a large heavy-duty saucepan over medium-high heat, stirring often. Bring the mixture to a boil, then reduce the heat as needed to maintain a steady boil and cook until the mixture reaches 300°F. You can swirl the mixture in the pan occasionally, but do not stir.

3. Remove from the heat and stir in the salt and vanilla.

4. Pour the contents onto the prepared jelly-roll pan. Let cool at room temperature for 2 to 3 hours.

5. Remove the cooled butterscotch from the pan and place on a cutting board. Cut or break it up into large chips. Store in an airtight container; the chips will keep for up to 2 weeks.

6. To make the cookies, cream the butter, brown sugar, and granulated sugar in a large mixing bowl until light and fluffy, about 2 minutes. Add the eggs, milk, and vanilla and beat until blended.

7. Whisk together the flour, baking powder, baking soda, and salt in a separate mixing bowl. Add to the butter mixture. Mix just until blended. Stir in the oats, followed by the butterscotch chips and walnuts.

8. Refrigerate the dough for at least 1 hour. In the meantime, preheat the oven to 350°F and grease two 14- by 16-inch cookie sheet pans. Note: unless you have a convection oven, which can handle multiple trays at once, bake only one sheet at a time.

9. Shape the cookies into balls: rounded teaspoons for small cookies, or rounded tablespoons for large ones. Place on baking sheets about 2 inches apart. Slightly flatten each ball into a disk.

10. Bake for 8 to 10 minutes, until the edges are slightly browned but the cookies are still white-ish.

11. Remove from the oven and let cool on the baking sheets for 5 minutes. Then transfer the cookies to baking racks to finish cooling.

Yield: about 75 small or
40 large cookies

Caramel Apples

The caramel coating on a caramel apple is soft, chewy, and sweet, the perfect complement to the crisp, tart apple. You can leave the caramel plain or roll the caramel-dipped apple in chopped or crushed nuts, sprinkles, crushed hard candies, cereal, or toffee bits. You will need sticks for dipping and holding the apples. The sticks are available at craft stores such as A.C. Moore, as well as online.

2 cups sugar

¼ cup light corn syrup

½ cup water

½ cup heavy cream

2 tablespoons unsalted butter

1 teaspoon vanilla extract

½ teaspoon sea salt

6 firm apples

1. Line a baking sheet with parchment paper, and spray the paper with cooking spray or lightly coat it with butter. Set aside.

2. Combine the sugar, corn syrup, and water in a heavy-duty saucepan over medium-high heat. Bring to a boil, stirring only until the sugar dissolves. Reduce the heat to maintain a steady boil and cook until the mixture is light amber in color and 300°F, 8 to 10 minutes. You can swirl the mixture in the pan, but do not stir.

3. Remove the pan from the heat and slowly whisk in the heavy cream. The mixture will bubble up quickly; keep whisking until it stops bubbling. Then add the butter, vanilla, and salt and whisk until smooth.

4. Insert a stick into the top of each apple, pushing it about halfway through. Dip the apples into the caramel, letting the excess drip off.

5. Set the apples on the prepared baking sheet. Let cool at room temperature.

Yield: 6 servings

Candy Apples

Candy apples, also called toffee apples, have a hard, crunchy exterior. This is essentially the transformation of an apple, one of the healthiest fruits on the planet, into a great candy. It's the best of both worlds. For a more festive look, you can add food coloring to the candy coating. Orange is a great color for a Halloween party, while the more traditional red works well for any time of year. You will need sticks for dipping and holding the apples.

> 2 cups sugar
>
> ¾ cup water
>
> ½ cup light corn syrup
>
> 8 drops food coloring, optional
>
> 6 apples

1. Line a baking sheet with parchment paper, and spray the paper with cooking spray or lightly coat it with butter. Set aside.

2. Combine the sugar, water, corn syrup, and food coloring, if using, in a heavy-duty saucepan. Bring to a boil, stirring only until the sugar dissolves. Reduce heat to maintain a steady boil and cook until the mixture reaches 300°F, about 20 minutes. You can swirl the mixture in the pan, but do not stir.

3. While the sugar is cooking, insert a wooden stick into the top of each apple, pushing it about halfway through.

4. When the sugar mixture reaches 300°F, immediately remove it from the heat. Carefully dip the apples into the very hot sugar mixture, letting the excess drip off.

5. Set the apples on the prepared baking sheet. Let cool at room temperature for about 20 minutes.

Yield: 6 servings

Caramelizing beyond Dessert

Thanks to their high levels of natural sugar, many vegetables will caramelize well. And unlike the other caramelizing in this book, you won't need ingredients such as butter, sugar, and cream, making this a healthful way to bring the joy of caramelizing into your kitchen.

Caramelizing onions — rendering them soft, browned, and sweet — is a slow process (usually at least 40 to 50 minutes), but it requires only minimal effort. Some shortcut recipes and enthusiastic TV shows have tried to convince home cooks that it takes only 20 to 30 minutes to caramelize onions. In that amount of time the onions may brown, or they may soften, but they won't do both. To make caramelized onions, start by peeling and thinly slicing 3 or 4 large onions. Heat a large skillet over medium heat and add 2 or 3 tablespoons of olive oil, the sliced onions, and a little salt and pepper. Stir the onions occasionally. Turn down the heat to medium-low

if they are becoming brown while still crunchy, and add a tablespoon or two of water if they are sticking to the bottom. Basically, you can leave them alone for most of the cooking and will end up with the perfect caramelized accompaniment to beef, pork, poultry, seafood, cheeses, sauces, quiches, and so much more.

I also love to roast root vegetables. The heat, along with a bit of fat (in this case olive oil), draws out the natural sugars. Good choices for caramelizing include onions, carrots, sweet potatoes, beets, parsnips, and radishes. You can combine them as you wish. Simply toss the peeled and chopped vegetables with olive oil, salt, pepper, and thyme (if desired) on a rimmed baking sheet and roast in a 400°F oven for about 45 minutes, or until the vegetables are cooked through and browned. Be sure to turn the vegetables every 10 to 12 minutes to prevent them from sticking to the pan. The resulting vegetables will be nicely browned, naturally sweet, and great tasting.

RESOURCES

SUPPLIES

Casco Bay Cutlery & Kitchenware
www.freeportknife.com

Williams-Sonoma
www.williams-sonoma.com

BOOKS AND WEBSITES

Arevalo, Sandy. *Artisan Caramels.*
Cedar Fort, 2014.

Gehring, Abigail R. *Classic Candy.*
Skyhorse Publishing, 2013.

Hermann, Martin K. *The Art of
Making Good Candies at Home.*
Doubleday, 1966.

LaBau, Elizabeth. *The Sweet Book
of Candymaking.* Quarry Books,
2012.

Brown Eyed Baker
www.browneyedbaker.com

David Lebovitz
www.davidlebovitz.com

The Kitchn
www.thekitchn.com

Metric Conversion Chart

Unless you have finely calibrated measuring equipment, conversions between U.S. and metric measurements will be somewhat inexact. It's important to convert the measurements for all of the ingredients in a recipe to maintain the same proportions as the original.

General Formula for Metric Conversion

Ounces to grams	multiply ounces by 28.35
Grams to ounces	multiply grams by 0.035
Pounds to grams	multiply pounds by 453.5
Pounds to kilograms	multiply pounds by 0.45
Cups to liters	multiply cups by 0.24
Fahrenheit to Celsius	subtract 32 from Fahrenheit temperature, multiply by 5, then divide by 9
Celsius to Fahrenheit	multiply Celsius temperature by 9, divide by 5, then add 32

Approximate Equivalent by Volume

U.S.	METRIC	U.S.	METRIC
1 teaspoon	5 milliliters	2 cups	460 milliliters
1 tablespoon	15 milliliters	4 cups (1 quart)	0.95 liter
½ cup	120 milliliters	1.06 quarts	1 liter
1 cup	230 milliliters		

Approximate Equivalent by Weight

U.S.	METRIC	METRIC	U.S.
½ ounce	14 grams	1 gram	0.035 ounce
1 ounce	28 grams	50 grams	1.75 ounces
1½ ounces	40 grams	100 grams	3.5 ounces
2½ ounces	70 grams	250 grams	8.75 ounces
4 ounces	112 grams	500 grams	1.1 pounds
8 ounces	228 grams	1 kilogram	2.2 pounds
16 ounces (1 pound)	454 grams		

INDEX

Page numbers in *italic* indicate illustrations; numbers in **bold** indicate charts.

OTHER STOREY BASICS® YOU WILL ENJOY

How to Make Chocolate Candies by Bill Collins
Chef Bill Collins teaches you how to temper chocolate, work with thickeners, boil sugar, and much more. With simple and delicious recipes like Peppermint Bark, Coffee Walnut Truffle, and Chocolate-Covered Candied Orange Peel, you can make your own homemade chocolate candy!
96 pages. Paper. ISBN 978-1-61212-357-8.

How to Make Frozen Yogurt by Nicole Weston
Enjoy your own homemade frozen yogurt with this innovative guide from food writer Nicole Weston. Produce 56 smooth and satisfying flavors such as Toasted Coconut, Chai Spice, White Chocolate Raspberry, Matcha Green Tea, and many more.
112 pages. Paper. ISBN 978-1-61212-377-6.

How to Make Ice Cream by Nicole Weston
Make your own delicious ice cream with this simple and thorough guide, which includes 50 enticing recipes such as Blackberry Cobbler, Peppermint Mocha, and Browned Butter.
96 pages. Paper. ISBN 978-1-61212-388-2.

Making Vegan Frozen Treats by Nicole Weston
Make rich, creamy desserts with your favorite soy, almond, or coconut milk. With over 50 recipes for ice creams, along with sorbets, granitas, and more from food blogger Nicole Weston, you can enjoy luscious and delicious dairy-free treats from your own kitchen.
96 pages. Paper. ISBN 978-1-61212-390-5.

These and other books from Storey Publishing are available wherever quality books are sold or by calling 1-800-441-5700. Visit us at *www.storey.com* or sign up for our newsletter at *www.storey.com/signup*.